FAMILY BUDGET
GOALS
&
FINANCIAL PLANNER

THIS BOOK BELONGS TO

_____

phone: _____

email: _____

CONTENTS

- ❖ Family Goals & Mission Statement
- ❖ Personal Net Worth Balance Sheet
- ❖ Important Account Information
- ❖ Insurance Policy Information
- ❖ Lump Sum Annual Payment Planner
- ❖ Annual Giving & Charity Tracker
- ❖ Visual Savings & Sinking Fund Tracker
- ❖ Debt Payoff Progress Tracker
- ❖ Bill Pay Tracker
- ❖ Quick Start Budget
- ❖ Monthly Budgeting Tools (18 months)
  - ➤ Zero-Based Monthly Budget Planner
  - ➤ Paycheck Budget Planner
  - ➤ Calendar Budget Planner
  - ➤ Dot-Grid Bullet Journaling Pages
- ❖ Full Year Calendars 2018-2022

FAMILY GOALS & MISSION STATEMENT

"A family mission statement is a combined, unified expression from all family members of what your family is all about —
what it is you really want to do and be — and the principles you choose to govern your family life."

-Stephen Covey

MISSION STATEMENT

_____

_____

_____

_____

"What you get by achieving your goals is not as important as what you become by achieving your goals."

-Zig Ziglar

SPIRITUAL

SOCIAL

FINANCIAL

MIND & INTELLECT

WORK & CAREER

PHYSICAL & HEALTH

FAMILY

Spiritual

Social

Financial

Family
Goals

Mind &
Intellect

Work &
Career

Physical
& Health

Family

Personal Net Worth & Balance Sheet Form

ASSETS	Value	Liabilities	Amount
Cash & Cash Equivalents		**Short-Term Credit**	
Cash on hand		Credit card 1	
Checking accounts		Credit card 2	
Savings account		Credit card 3	
Money Market		Credit card 4	
Certificates of Deposit (CD's)		Loans from friends/family	
Other 1		Home line of credit	
Total Cash & Cash Equivalents		Other 1	
		Total Short Term Credit	
Brokerage Accounts			
Stocks		**Loans & Mortgages**	
Mutual Funds		Primary Residence	
Municipal bonds		Secondary Residence	
Government bonds		Rental Property	
Corporate bonds		Investment Property	
Other 1		Vehicle 1	
Other 2		Vehicle 2	
Total Brokerage Accounts		Recreational vehicle 1	
		Recreational vehicle 2	
Retirement Accounts		Student Loans	
401(K)		Business Loans	
403(b)		401(k) Loans	
457(b)		Other 1	
IRA - Roth		**Total Loans & Mortgages**	
IRA - Traditional			
Profit Sharing		**Other Liabilities**	
Pension		Medical Debts	
Total Retirement Accounts		Commitments to donate	
		Other 1	
Other Savings Accounts		Other 2	
College 529 Plan		Other 3	
Health Savings Account (HSA)		**Total Other Liabilities**	
Cash Value (Insurance)			
Total Other Savings Accounts		**Total Liabilities**	
Property		**Current Net Worth**	
Primary Residence		**= Assets - Liabilities**	
Secondary Residence			
Rental Property		**Net Worth Over Time**	
Investment Property			
Vehicle 1			
Vehicle 2		Year 1	
Recreational vehicle 1		Year 2	
Recreational vehicle 2		Year 3	
Jewelry		Year 4	
Antiques		Year 5	
Other		**NOTES**	
Total Property			
Total Assets			

IMPORTANT ACCOUNT INFORMATION

KEEP IN A SECURE LOCATION

Account Type	
Website	
Account #	
Login	
Password	
Other:	

Account Type	
Website	
Account #	
Login	
Password	
Other:	

Account Type	
Website	
Account #	
Login	
Password	
Other:	

Account Type	
Website	
Account #	
Login	
Password	
Other:	

Account Type	
Website	
Account #	
Login	
Password	
Other:	

Account Type	
Website	
Account #	
Login	
Password	
Other:	

Account Type	
Website	
Account #	
Login	
Password	
Other:	

Account Type	
Website	
Account #	
Login	
Password	
Other:	

Account Type	
Website	
Account #	
Login	
Password	
Other:	

Account Type	
Website	
Account #	
Login	
Password	
Other:	

INSURANCE POLICY INFORMATION

Policy Type	
Provider	
Policy #	
Phone Number	
Agent	
Deductible	
Policy Notes	

Policy Type	
Provider	
Policy #	
Phone Number	
Agent	
Deductible	
Policy Notes	

Policy Type	
Provider	
Policy #	
Phone Number	
Agent	
Deductible	
Policy Notes	

Policy Type	
Provider	
Policy #	
Phone Number	
Agent	
Deductible	
Policy Notes	

Policy Type	
Provider	
Policy #	
Phone Number	
Agent	
Deductible	
Policy Notes	

Policy Type	
Provider	
Policy #	
Phone Number	
Agent	
Deductible	
Policy Notes	

Policy Type	
Provider	
Policy #	
Phone Number	
Agent	
Deductible	
Policy Notes	

Policy Type	
Provider	
Policy #	
Phone Number	
Agent	
Deductible	
Policy Notes	

Annual Giving & Charity Tracker

Year: _____

Goal for the Year: _____

January

Date	Charity	Amount	Note
Total:			

February

Date	Charity	Amount	Note
Total:			

March

Date	Charity	Amount	Note
Total:			

April

Date	Charity	Amount	Note
Total:			

May

Date	Charity	Amount	Note
Total:			

June

Date	Charity	Amount	Note
Total:			

July

Date	Charity	Amount	Note
Total:			

August

Date	Charity	Amount	Note
Total:			

September

Date	Charity	Amount	Note
Total:			

October

Date	Charity	Amount	Note
Total:			

November

Date	Charity	Amount	Note
Total:			

December

Date	Charity	Amount	Note
Total:			

Total Giving for the Year:_____

Lump Sum Infrequent Payment Planner

Use this tool to help plan for expenses that are infrequent and not paid monthly.

Expense	Expected Due Date	Amount	÷	Months Until Due	=	Monthly Budget
Real Estate Taxes						
Homeowners Insurance						
HOA Fees						
Home Repairs						
Car Insurance						
Car Repairs						
Car Tags/Registration						
Car Replacement						
School Fees						
School Tuition						
IRS (Self Employed)						
Vacation						
Gifts (incl. Christmas)						
Back to School Supplies						
Club Dues						
Annual Subscriptions						
Other						
Other						
Other						
Other						
Other						
Other						

Visual Savings & Sinking Fund Tracker

Track your progress on savings! Set a goal, divide it into smaller steps and then shade in the boxes as you meet certain milestones!

| SAVINGS: | *Emergency Fund* | GOAL: | $1,000 |

$50	$150	$250	$350	$450	$550	$650	$750	$850	$950
$100	$200	$300	$400	$500	$600	$700	$800	$900	$1000

| SAVINGS: | | GOAL: | |

| SAVINGS: | | GOAL: | |

| SAVINGS: | | GOAL: | |

| SAVINGS: | | GOAL: | |

| SAVINGS: | | GOAL: | |

| SAVINGS: | | GOAL: | |

| SAVINGS: | | GOAL: | |

| SAVINGS: | | GOAL: | |

BILL PAY TRACKER

Keep track of when you have paid your bills and never forget another payment.
List your bills in the order that they are due throughout the month.
Keep track of the Method: A=Auto Deduct, M=Manually Online, CK=Check, C=Cash

BILL	DUE DATE	AMOUNT	METHOD	MONTH																						

Monthly Debt Balance Payoff Progress Tracker

The best approach to be debt free quickly is to attack your debts smallest to largest.
Apply extra payments on your lowest debt to pay it off and build your "debt snowball".

Debt List (Smallest to Largest)	Starting Balance	Minimum Payment	MONTH									
			Jan-18	Feb-18	Mar-18	Apr-18	May-18	Jun-18	Jul-18	Aug-18	Sep-18	Oct-18
EXAMPLE: VISA CC	$1,250	$75	$1,189	$1,105	$990	$880	$650	$400	$310	$190	$100	$0 !!!

BASIC. SIMPLE. QUICK START BUDGET

Use this form to get started on your first budget. This is a plan for your money.

"A budget is telling your money where to go instead of wondering where it went." - Dave Ramsey

STEP 1 | Income Sources
What is your "Take-Home" Pay after taxes?

Income	Amount per month
Paycheck 1:	
Paycheck 2:	
Other:	
Other:	
Other:	
TOTAL MONTHLY INCOME:	

STEP 2 | Basic Living Expenses
These are your "Four Walls" - Basic Necessities

	Expense	Amount per month
Food	Groceries	
	Restaurants	
Shelter	1st Mortgage / Rent	
	2nd Mortgage	
	Home/Rental Insurance	
	Property Taxes	
Utilities	Power/Electricity	
	Gas	
	Trash	
	Water	
Transportation	Fuel	
	Tolls/Parking	
	Car Insurance	
	Tags/Registration	
	TOTAL BASIC EXPENSES:	

STEP 3 | Other Living Expenses
What else do you spend money on?

Expense	Amount per month
Clothing	
Phone	
Internet	
Home Repairs	
Car Repairs	
Entertainment	
Life Insurance	
Child Care	
Gifts (Incl. Christmas)	
Education / Tuition	
Subscriptions	
Other:	
Other:	
Other:	
Other:	
TOTAL OTHER EXPENSES:	

STEP 4 | Charity & Giving

What are you giving or donating?	Amount per month
TOTAL GIVING:	

STEP 5 | SAVINGS

What are you saving?	Amount per month
TOTAL SAVINGS:	

STEP 6 | Debts
What are your non-mortgage debts smallest to largest?

Debt	Balance	Minimum Payment
TOTAL DEBT MONTHLY PAYMENTS:		

STEP 7: Calculate Total Income, Total Expenses & End of Month Balance

TOTAL INCOME		TOTAL EXPENSES	
What is your total income? (Step 1)		What are your total expenses? (Steps 2-6)	

END OF MONTH BALANCE = TOTAL INCOME - TOTAL EXPENSES	

Your Goal should be a ZERO-BASED BUDGET with End of Month Balance = $0.
Every dollar has an assignment and a job to do throughout the month.

Monthly Zero-Based Budget Planner

Start with a FRESH budget each month!

Month:	
Year:	

> Use the Quick Start Budget to help get started but be sure to plan for the special expenses that you will incur this month.
> Use the Paycheck Budget Planner to help plan out your cash flow and which expenses will be covered by each paycheck.
> Use the Calendar Budget Planner to map out a visual of when your income and expenses will occur throughout the month.

Income	Date	Planned	Actual
Total Income:			

NOTES

Basic Living Expenses			
Expense	Date	Planned	Actual
Food			
Home			
Utilities			
Transportation			
Total Basic Expenses			

Other Expenses			
Expense	Date	Planned	Actual
Giving			
Savings			
Other			
Debts			
Total Other Expenses			

Zero-Based Budget: A plan for every dollar

Total Income = Total Expenses

Any extra money in the budget should be applied towards debt, savings, and other goals that you have set.

Debt Snapshot	
Starting Balance	
Ending Balance	
Paid Off:	

Savings Snapshot	
Starting Balance	
Ending Balance	
Total Saved:	

PAYCHECK BUDGET

Useful for cashflow planning. Plan your expenses to be covered by certain paychecks to have an even cashflow throughout the month.

MONTH: **YEAR:**

Income	Exp. Date	Expected Amount	Actual	Difference
Paycheck 1				
Paycheck 2				
Paycheck 3				
Total Income:				

Paycheck 1 Expenses	Due Date	Budget	Actual	Difference
Subtotal Expenses:				

Paycheck 2 Expenses	Due Date	Budget	Actual	Difference
Subtotal Expenses:				

Paycheck 3 Expenses	Due Date	Budget	Actual	Difference
Subtotal Expenses:				
Total Expenses (All Subtotals):				
Month End Balance (=Income - Expenses):				

CALENDAR BUDGET

MONTH: | **YEAR:**

SUNDAY	MONDAY	TUESDAY	WEDNESDAY
BALANCE:	BALANCE:	BALANCE:	BALANCE:
BALANCE:	BALANCE:	BALANCE:	BALANCE:
BALANCE:	BALANCE:	BALANCE:	BALANCE:
BALANCE:	BALANCE:	BALANCE:	BALANCE:
BALANCE:	BALANCE:	BALANCE:	BALANCE:

Useful for cashflow planning. Plan your income and major bills & expenses throughout the month and record your daily projected balances to ensure you have a balanced budget.

NOTES

THURSDAY	FRIDAY	SATURDAY
BALANCE:	BALANCE:	BALANCE:
BALANCE:	BALANCE:	BALANCE:
BALANCE:	BALANCE:	BALANCE:
BALANCE:	BALANCE:	BALANCE:
BALANCE:	BALANCE:	BALANCE:

Monthly Zero-Based Budget Planner

Start with a FRESH budget each month!

Month:

Year:

>Use the Quick Start Budget to help get started but be sure to plan for the special expenses that you will incur this month.
>Use the Paycheck Budget Planner to help plan out your cash flow and which expenses will be covered by each paycheck.
>Use the Calendar Budget Planner to map out a visual of when your income and expenses will occur throughout the month.

Income	Date	Planned	Actual
Total Income:			

NOTES

Basic Living Expenses					Other Expenses			
Expense	**Date**	**Planned**	**Actual**		**Expense**	**Date**	**Planned**	**Actual**
Food					Giving			
					Savings			
Home					Other			
Utilities								
Transportation					Debts			
Total Basic Expenses								

Zero-Based Budget: A plan for every dollar

Total Income = Total Expenses

Any extra money in the budget should be applied towards debt, savings, and other goals that you have set.

Total Other Expenses		

Debt Snapshot	
Starting Balance	
Ending Balance	
Paid Off:	

Savings Snapshot	
Starting Balance	
Ending Balance	
Total Saved:	

PAYCHECK BUDGET

Useful for cashflow planning. Plan your expenses to be covered by certain paychecks to have an even cashflow throughout the month.

MONTH:

YEAR:

Income	Exp. Date	Expected Amount	Actual	Difference
Paycheck 1				
Paycheck 2				
Paycheck 3				
Total Income:				

Paycheck 1 Expenses	Due Date	Budget	Actual	Difference
Subtotal Expenses:				

Paycheck 2 Expenses	Due Date	Budget	Actual	Difference
Subtotal Expenses:				

Paycheck 3 Expenses	Due Date	Budget	Actual	Difference
Subtotal Expenses:				

Total Expenses (All Subtotals):				
Month End Balance (=Income - Expenses):				

CALENDAR BUDGET

MONTH:		YEAR:	
SUNDAY	**MONDAY**	**TUESDAY**	**WEDNESDAY**
BALANCE:	BALANCE:	BALANCE:	BALANCE:
BALANCE:	BALANCE:	BALANCE:	BALANCE:
BALANCE:	BALANCE:	BALANCE:	BALANCE:
BALANCE:	BALANCE:	BALANCE:	BALANCE:
BALANCE:	BALANCE:	BALANCE:	BALANCE:

Useful for cashflow planning. Plan your income and major bills & expenses throughout the month and record your daily projected balances to ensure you have a balanced budget.

NOTES

THURSDAY	FRIDAY	SATURDAY
BALANCE:	BALANCE:	BALANCE:
BALANCE:	BALANCE:	BALANCE:
BALANCE:	BALANCE:	BALANCE:
BALANCE:	BALANCE:	BALANCE:
BALANCE:	BALANCE:	BALANCE:

Monthly Zero-Based Budget Planner

Start with a FRESH budget each month!

Month:

Year:

>Use the Quick Start Budget to help get started but be sure to plan for the special expenses that you will incur this month.
>Use the Paycheck Budget Planner to help plan out your cash flow and which expenses will be covered by each paycheck.
>Use the Calendar Budget Planner to map out a visual of when your income and expenses will occur throughout the month.

Income	Date	Planned	Actual
Total Income:			

NOTES

Basic Living Expenses			
Expense	Date	Planned	Actual
Food			
Home			
Utilities			
Transportation			
Total Basic Expenses			

Other Expenses			
Expense	Date	Planned	Actual
Giving			
Savings			
Other			
Debts			
Total Other Expenses			

Zero-Based Budget: A plan for every dollar

Total Income = Total Expenses

Any extra money in the budget should be applied towards debt, savings, and other goals that you have set.

Debt Snapshot

Starting Balance	
Ending Balance	
Paid Off:	

Savings Snapshot

Starting Balance	
Ending Balance	
Total Saved:	

PAYCHECK BUDGET

Useful for cashflow planning. Plan your expenses to be covered by certain paychecks to have an even cashflow throughout the month.

MONTH: **YEAR:**

Income	Exp. Date	Expected Amount	Actual	Difference
Paycheck 1				
Paycheck 2				
Paycheck 3				
Total Income:				

Paycheck 1 Expenses	Due Date	Budget	Actual	Difference
Subtotal Expenses:				

Paycheck 2 Expenses	Due Date	Budget	Actual	Difference
Subtotal Expenses:				

Paycheck 3 Expenses	Due Date	Budget	Actual	Difference
Subtotal Expenses:				
Total Expenses (All Subtotals):				
Month End Balance (=Income - Expenses):				

CALENDAR BUDGET

MONTH: **YEAR:**

SUNDAY	MONDAY	TUESDAY	WEDNESDAY
BALANCE:	BALANCE:	BALANCE:	BALANCE:
BALANCE:	BALANCE:	BALANCE:	BALANCE:
BALANCE:	BALANCE:	BALANCE:	BALANCE:
BALANCE:	BALANCE:	BALANCE:	BALANCE:
BALANCE:	BALANCE:	BALANCE:	BALANCE:

Useful for cashflow planning. Plan your income and major bills & expenses throughout the month and record your daily projected balances to ensure you have a balanced budget.

NOTES

THURSDAY	FRIDAY	SATURDAY
BALANCE:	BALANCE:	BALANCE:
BALANCE:	BALANCE:	BALANCE:
BALANCE:	BALANCE:	BALANCE:
BALANCE:	BALANCE:	BALANCE:
BALANCE:	BALANCE:	BALANCE:

Monthly Zero-Based Budget Planner
Start with a FRESH budget each month!

Month:	
Year:	

>Use the Quick Start Budget to help get started but be sure to plan for the special expenses that you will incur this month.
>Use the Paycheck Budget Planner to help plan out your cash flow and which expenses will be covered by each paycheck.
>Use the Calendar Budget Planner to map out a visual of when your income and expenses will occur throughout the month.

Income	Date	Planned	Actual
Total Income:			

NOTES

Basic Living Expenses			
Expense	**Date**	**Planned**	**Actual**
Food			
Home			
Utilities			
Transportation			
Total Basic Expenses			

Other Expenses			
Expense	**Date**	**Planned**	**Actual**
Giving			
Savings			
Other			
Debts			
Total Other Expenses			

Zero-Based Budget: A plan for every dollar

Total Income = Total Expenses

Any extra money in the budget should be applied towards debt, savings, and other goals that you have set.

Debt Snapshot	
Starting Balance	
Ending Balance	
Paid Off:	

Savings Snapshot	
Starting Balance	
Ending Balance	
Total Saved:	

PAYCHECK BUDGET		Useful for cashflow planning. Plan your expenses to be covered by certain paychecks to have an even cashflow throughout the month.		
MONTH:		**YEAR:**		
Income	**Exp. Date**	**Expected Amount**	**Actual**	**Difference**
Paycheck 1				
Paycheck 2				
Paycheck 3				
Total Income:				
Paycheck 1 Expenses	**Due Date**	**Budget**	**Actual**	**Difference**
Subtotal Expenses:				
Paycheck 2 Expenses	**Due Date**	**Budget**	**Actual**	**Difference**
Subtotal Expenses:				
Paycheck 3 Expenses	**Due Date**	**Budget**	**Actual**	**Difference**
Subtotal Expenses:				
Total Expenses (All Subtotals):				
Month End Balance (=Income - Expenses):				

CALENDAR BUDGET

MONTH:

YEAR:

SUNDAY	MONDAY	TUESDAY	WEDNESDAY
BALANCE:	BALANCE:	BALANCE:	BALANCE:
BALANCE:	BALANCE:	BALANCE:	BALANCE:
BALANCE:	BALANCE:	BALANCE:	BALANCE:
BALANCE:	BALANCE:	BALANCE:	BALANCE:
BALANCE:	BALANCE:	BALANCE:	BALANCE:

Useful for cashflow planning. Plan your income and major bills & expenses throughout the month and record your daily projected balances to ensure you have a balanced budget.

NOTES

THURSDAY	FRIDAY	SATURDAY
BALANCE:	BALANCE:	BALANCE:
BALANCE:	BALANCE:	BALANCE:
BALANCE:	BALANCE:	BALANCE:
BALANCE:	BALANCE:	BALANCE:
BALANCE:	BALANCE:	BALANCE:

Monthly Zero-Based Budget Planner
Start with a FRESH budget each month!

Month:

Year:

>Use the Quick Start Budget to help get started but be sure to plan for the special expenses that you will incur this month.
>Use the Paycheck Budget Planner to help plan out your cash flow and which expenses will be covered by each paycheck.
>Use the Calendar Budget Planner to map out a visual of when your income and expenses will occur throughout the month.

Income	Date	Planned	Actual
Total Income:			

NOTES

Basic Living Expenses

Expense	Date	Planned	Actual
Food			
Home			
Utilities			
Transportation			
Total Basic Expenses			

Other Expenses

Expense	Date	Planned	Actual
Giving			
Savings			
Other			
Debts			
Total Other Expenses			

Zero-Based Budget: A plan for every dollar

Total Income = Total Expenses

Any extra money in the budget should be applied towards debt, savings, and other goals that you have set.

Debt Snapshot

Starting Balance	
Ending Balance	
Paid Off:	

Savings Snapshot

Starting Balance	
Ending Balance	
Total Saved:	

PAYCHECK BUDGET

Useful for cashflow planning. Plan your expenses to be covered by certain paychecks to have an even cashflow throughout the month.

MONTH:

YEAR:

Income	Exp. Date	Expected Amount	Actual	Difference
Paycheck 1				
Paycheck 2				
Paycheck 3				
Total Income:				

Paycheck 1 Expenses	Due Date	Budget	Actual	Difference
Subtotal Expenses:				

Paycheck 2 Expenses	Due Date	Budget	Actual	Difference
Subtotal Expenses:				

Paycheck 3 Expenses	Due Date	Budget	Actual	Difference
Subtotal Expenses:				

Total Expenses (All Subtotals):				
Month End Balance (=Income - Expenses):				

CALENDAR BUDGET

MONTH:

YEAR:

SUNDAY	MONDAY	TUESDAY	WEDNESDAY
BALANCE:	BALANCE:	BALANCE:	BALANCE:
BALANCE:	BALANCE:	BALANCE:	BALANCE:
BALANCE:	BALANCE:	BALANCE:	BALANCE:
BALANCE:	BALANCE:	BALANCE:	BALANCE:
BALANCE:	BALANCE:	BALANCE:	BALANCE:

Useful for cashflow planning. Plan your income and major bills & expenses throughout the month and record your daily projected balances to ensure you have a balanced budget.

NOTES

THURSDAY	FRIDAY	SATURDAY
BALANCE:	BALANCE:	BALANCE:
BALANCE:	BALANCE:	BALANCE:
BALANCE:	BALANCE:	BALANCE:
BALANCE:	BALANCE:	BALANCE:
BALANCE:	BALANCE:	BALANCE:

Monthly Zero-Based Budget Planner
Start with a FRESH budget each month!

Month:	
Year:	

>Use the Quick Start Budget to help get started but be sure to plan for the special expenses that you will incur this month.
>Use the Paycheck Budget Planner to help plan out your cash flow and which expenses will be covered by each paycheck.
>Use the Calendar Budget Planner to map out a visual of when your income and expenses will occur throughout the month.

Income	Date	Planned	Actual
Total Income:			

NOTES

Basic Living Expenses			
Expense	Date	Planned	Actual
Food			
Home			
Utilities			
Transportation			
Total Basic Expenses			

Other Expenses			
Expense	Date	Planned	Actual
Giving			
Savings			
Other			
Debts			
Total Other Expenses		

Zero-Based Budget: A plan for every dollar

Total Income = Total Expenses

Any extra money in the budget should be applied towards debt, savings, and other goals that you have set.

Debt Snapshot	
Starting Balance	
Ending Balance	
Paid Off:	

Savings Snapshot	
Starting Balance	
Ending Balance	
Total Saved:	

PAYCHECK BUDGET

Useful for cashflow planning. Plan your expenses to be covered by certain paychecks to have an even cashflow throughout the month.

MONTH: **YEAR:**

Income	Exp. Date	Expected Amount	Actual	Difference
Paycheck 1				
Paycheck 2				
Paycheck 3				
Total Income:				

Paycheck 1 Expenses	Due Date	Budget	Actual	Difference
Subtotal Expenses:				

Paycheck 2 Expenses	Due Date	Budget	Actual	Difference
Subtotal Expenses:				

Paycheck 3 Expenses	Due Date	Budget	Actual	Difference
Subtotal Expenses:				
Total Expenses (All Subtotals):				
Month End Balance (=Income - Expenses):				

CALENDAR BUDGET

MONTH:

YEAR:

SUNDAY	MONDAY	TUESDAY	WEDNESDAY
BALANCE:	BALANCE:	BALANCE:	BALANCE:
BALANCE:	BALANCE:	BALANCE:	BALANCE:
BALANCE:	BALANCE:	BALANCE:	BALANCE:
BALANCE:	BALANCE:	BALANCE:	BALANCE:
BALANCE:	BALANCE:	BALANCE:	BALANCE:

Useful for cashflow planning. Plan your income and major bills & expenses throughout the month and record your daily projected balances to ensure you have a balanced budget.

THURSDAY	FRIDAY	SATURDAY
BALANCE:	BALANCE:	BALANCE:
BALANCE:	BALANCE:	BALANCE:
BALANCE:	BALANCE:	BALANCE:
BALANCE:	BALANCE:	BALANCE:
BALANCE:	BALANCE:	BALANCE:

Monthly Zero-Based Budget Planner
Start with a FRESH budget each month!

Month:	
Year:	

>Use the Quick Start Budget to help get started but be sure to plan for the special expenses that you will incur this month.
>Use the Paycheck Budget Planner to help plan out your cash flow and which expenses will be covered by each paycheck.
>Use the Calendar Budget Planner to map out a visual of when your income and expenses will occur throughout the month.

Income	Date	Planned	Actual
Total Income:			

NOTES

Basic Living Expenses

Expense	Date	Planned	Actual
Food			
Home			
Utilities			
Transportation			
Total Basic Expenses			

Other Expenses

Expense	Date	Planned	Actual
Giving			
Savings			
Other			
Debts			
Total Other Expenses		

Zero-Based Budget: A plan for every dollar

Total Income = Total Expenses

Any extra money in the budget should be applied towards debt, savings, and other goals that you have set.

Debt Snapshot

Starting Balance	
Ending Balance	
Paid Off:	

Savings Snapshot

Starting Balance	
Ending Balance	
Total Saved:	

PAYCHECK BUDGET

Useful for cashflow planning. Plan your expenses to be covered by certain paychecks to have an even cashflow throughout the month.

MONTH: **YEAR:**

Income	Exp. Date	Expected Amount	Actual	Difference
Paycheck 1				
Paycheck 2				
Paycheck 3				
Total Income:				

Paycheck 1 Expenses	Due Date	Budget	Actual	Difference
Subtotal Expenses:				

Paycheck 2 Expenses	Due Date	Budget	Actual	Difference
Subtotal Expenses:				

Paycheck 3 Expenses	Due Date	Budget	Actual	Difference
Subtotal Expenses:				

| **Total Expenses (All Subtotals):** | | | | |
| **Month End Balance (=Income - Expenses):** | | | | |

CALENDAR BUDGET

MONTH: **YEAR:**

SUNDAY	MONDAY	TUESDAY	WEDNESDAY
BALANCE:	BALANCE:	BALANCE:	BALANCE:
BALANCE:	BALANCE:	BALANCE:	BALANCE:
BALANCE:	BALANCE:	BALANCE:	BALANCE:
BALANCE:	BALANCE:	BALANCE:	BALANCE:
BALANCE:	BALANCE:	BALANCE:	BALANCE:

Useful for cashflow planning. Plan your income and major bills & expenses throughout the month and record your daily projected balances to ensure you have a balanced budget.

NOTES

THURSDAY	FRIDAY	SATURDAY
BALANCE:	BALANCE:	BALANCE:
BALANCE:	BALANCE:	BALANCE:
BALANCE:	BALANCE:	BALANCE:
BALANCE:	BALANCE:	BALANCE:
BALANCE:	BALANCE:	BALANCE:

Monthly Zero-Based Budget Planner

Start with a FRESH budget each month!

Month:	
Year:	

>Use the Quick Start Budget to help get started but be sure to plan for the special expenses that you will incur this month.
>Use the Paycheck Budget Planner to help plan out your cash flow and which expenses will be covered by each paycheck.
>Use the Calendar Budget Planner to map out a visual of when your income and expenses will occur throughout the month.

Income	Date	Planned	Actual
Total Income:			

NOTES

Basic Living Expenses

Expense	Date	Planned	Actual
Food			
Home			
Utilities			
Transportation			
Total Basic Expenses			

Other Expenses

Expense	Date	Planned	Actual
Giving			
Savings			
Other			
Debts			
Total Other Expenses		

Zero-Based Budget: A plan for every dollar

Total Income = Total Expenses

Any extra money in the budget should be applied towards debt, savings, and other goals that you have set.

Debt Snapshot

Starting Balance	
Ending Balance	
Paid Off:	

Savings Snapshot

Starting Balance	
Ending Balance	
Total Saved:	

PAYCHECK BUDGET

Useful for cashflow planning. Plan your expenses to be covered by certain paychecks to have an even cashflow throughout the month.

MONTH: **YEAR:**

Income	Exp. Date	Expected Amount	Actual	Difference
Paycheck 1				
Paycheck 2				
Paycheck 3				
Total Income:				

Paycheck 1 Expenses	Due Date	Budget	Actual	Difference
Subtotal Expenses:				

Paycheck 2 Expenses	Due Date	Budget	Actual	Difference
Subtotal Expenses:				

Paycheck 3 Expenses	Due Date	Budget	Actual	Difference
Subtotal Expenses:				

Total Expenses (All Subtotals):				
Month End Balance (=Income - Expenses):				

CALENDAR BUDGET

MONTH: **YEAR:**

SUNDAY	MONDAY	TUESDAY	WEDNESDAY
BALANCE:	BALANCE:	BALANCE:	BALANCE:
BALANCE:	BALANCE:	BALANCE:	BALANCE:
BALANCE:	BALANCE:	BALANCE:	BALANCE:
BALANCE:	BALANCE:	BALANCE:	BALANCE:
BALANCE:	BALANCE:	BALANCE:	BALANCE:

Useful for cashflow planning. Plan your income and major bills & expenses throughout the month and record your daily projected balances to ensure you have a balanced budget.

NOTES

THURSDAY	FRIDAY	SATURDAY
BALANCE:	BALANCE:	BALANCE:
BALANCE:	BALANCE:	BALANCE:
BALANCE:	BALANCE:	BALANCE:
BALANCE:	BALANCE:	BALANCE:
BALANCE:	BALANCE:	BALANCE:

Monthly Zero-Based Budget Planner
Start with a FRESH budget each month!

Month:	
Year:	

>Use the Quick Start Budget to help get started but be sure to plan for the special expenses that you will incur this month.
>Use the Paycheck Budget Planner to help plan out your cash flow and which expenses will be covered by each paycheck.
>Use the Calendar Budget Planner to map out a visual of when your income and expenses will occur throughout the month.

Income	Date	Planned	Actual
Total Income:			

NOTES

Basic Living Expenses			
Expense	Date	Planned	Actual
Food			
Home			
Utilities			
Transportation			
Total Basic Expenses			

Other Expenses			
Expense	Date	Planned	Actual
Giving			
Savings			
Other			
Debts			
Total Other Expenses			

Zero-Based Budget: A plan for every dollar

Total Income = Total Expenses

Any extra money in the budget should be applied towards debt, savings, and other goals that you have set.

Debt Snapshot	
Starting Balance	
Ending Balance	
Paid Off:	

Savings Snapshot	
Starting Balance	
Ending Balance	
Total Saved:	

PAYCHECK BUDGET

Useful for cashflow planning. Plan your expenses to be covered by certain paychecks to have an even cashflow throughout the month.

MONTH: **YEAR:**

Income	Exp. Date	Expected Amount	Actual	Difference
Paycheck 1				
Paycheck 2				
Paycheck 3				
Total Income:				

Paycheck 1 Expenses	Due Date	Budget	Actual	Difference
Subtotal Expenses:				

Paycheck 2 Expenses	Due Date	Budget	Actual	Difference
Subtotal Expenses:				

Paycheck 3 Expenses	Due Date	Budget	Actual	Difference
Subtotal Expenses:				
Total Expenses (All Subtotals):				
Month End Balance (=Income - Expenses):				

CALENDAR BUDGET

MONTH: **YEAR:**

SUNDAY	MONDAY	TUESDAY	WEDNESDAY
BALANCE:	BALANCE:	BALANCE:	BALANCE:
BALANCE:	BALANCE:	BALANCE:	BALANCE:
BALANCE:	BALANCE:	BALANCE:	BALANCE:
BALANCE:	BALANCE:	BALANCE:	BALANCE:
BALANCE:	BALANCE:	BALANCE:	BALANCE:

Useful for cashflow planning. Plan your income and major bills & expenses throughout the month and record your daily projected balances to ensure you have a balanced budget.

NOTES

THURSDAY	FRIDAY	SATURDAY
BALANCE:	BALANCE:	BALANCE:
BALANCE:	BALANCE:	BALANCE:
BALANCE:	BALANCE:	BALANCE:
BALANCE:	BALANCE:	BALANCE:
BALANCE:	BALANCE:	BALANCE:

Monthly Zero-Based Budget Planner

Start with a FRESH budget each month!

Month:	
Year:	

>Use the Quick Start Budget to help get started but be sure to plan for the special expenses that you will incur this month.
>Use the Paycheck Budget Planner to help plan out your cash flow and which expenses will be covered by each paycheck.
>Use the Calendar Budget Planner to map out a visual of when your income and expenses will occur throughout the month.

Income	Date	Planned	Actual
Total Income:			

NOTES

Basic Living Expenses

Expense	Date	Planned	Actual
Food			
Home			
Utilities			
Transportation			
Total Basic Expenses			

Zero-Based Budget: A plan for every dollar

Total Income = Total Expenses

Any extra money in the budget should be applied towards debt, savings, and other goals that you have set.

Other Expenses

Expense	Date	Planned	Actual
Giving			
Savings			
Other			
Debts			
Total Other Expenses			

Debt Snapshot

Starting Balance	
Ending Balance	
Paid Off:	

Savings Snapshot

Starting Balance	
Ending Balance	
Total Saved:	

PAYCHECK BUDGET

Useful for cashflow planning. Plan your expenses to be covered by certain paychecks to have an even cashflow throughout the month.

MONTH: **YEAR:**

Income	Exp. Date	Expected Amount	Actual	Difference
Paycheck 1				
Paycheck 2				
Paycheck 3				
Total Income:				

Paycheck 1 Expenses	Due Date	Budget	Actual	Difference
Subtotal Expenses:				

Paycheck 2 Expenses	Due Date	Budget	Actual	Difference
Subtotal Expenses:				

Paycheck 3 Expenses	Due Date	Budget	Actual	Difference
Subtotal Expenses:				
Total Expenses (All Subtotals):				
Month End Balance (=Income - Expenses):				

CALENDAR BUDGET

MONTH: **YEAR:**

SUNDAY	MONDAY	TUESDAY	WEDNESDAY
BALANCE:	BALANCE:	BALANCE:	BALANCE:
BALANCE:	BALANCE:	BALANCE:	BALANCE:
BALANCE:	BALANCE:	BALANCE:	BALANCE:
BALANCE:	BALANCE:	BALANCE:	BALANCE:
BALANCE:	BALANCE:	BALANCE:	BALANCE:

Useful for cashflow planning. Plan your income and major bills & expenses throughout the month and record your daily projected balances to ensure you have a balanced budget.

NOTES

THURSDAY	FRIDAY	SATURDAY
BALANCE:	BALANCE:	BALANCE:
BALANCE:	BALANCE:	BALANCE:
BALANCE:	BALANCE:	BALANCE:
BALANCE:	BALANCE:	BALANCE:
BALANCE:	BALANCE:	BALANCE:

Monthly Zero-Based Budget Planner

Start with a FRESH budget each month!

Month:	
Year:	

>Use the Quick Start Budget to help get started but be sure to plan for the special expenses that you will incur this month.
>Use the Paycheck Budget Planner to help plan out your cash flow and which expenses will be covered by each paycheck.
>Use the Calendar Budget Planner to map out a visual of when your income and expenses will occur throughout the month.

Income	Date	Planned	Actual
Total Income:			

NOTES

Basic Living Expenses

Expense	Date	Planned	Actual
Food			
Home			
Utilities			
Transportation			
Total Basic Expenses			

Other Expenses

Expense	Date	Planned	Actual
Giving			
Savings			
Other			
Debts			
Total Other Expenses			

Zero-Based Budget: A plan for every dollar

Total Income = Total Expenses

Any extra money in the budget should be applied towards debt, savings, and other goals that you have set.

Debt Snapshot

Starting Balance	
Ending Balance	
Paid Off:	

Savings Snapshot

Starting Balance	
Ending Balance	
Total Saved:	

PAYCHECK BUDGET

Useful for cashflow planning. Plan your expenses to be covered by certain paychecks to have an even cashflow throughout the month.

MONTH: | **YEAR:**

Income	Exp. Date	Expected Amount	Actual	Difference
Paycheck 1				
Paycheck 2				
Paycheck 3				
Total Income:				

Paycheck 1 Expenses	Due Date	Budget	Actual	Difference
Subtotal Expenses:				

Paycheck 2 Expenses	Due Date	Budget	Actual	Difference
Subtotal Expenses:				

Paycheck 3 Expenses	Due Date	Budget	Actual	Difference
Subtotal Expenses:				

Total Expenses (All Subtotals):				
Month End Balance (=Income - Expenses):				

CALENDAR BUDGET

MONTH:

YEAR:

SUNDAY	MONDAY	TUESDAY	WEDNESDAY
BALANCE:	BALANCE:	BALANCE:	BALANCE:
BALANCE:	BALANCE:	BALANCE:	BALANCE:
BALANCE:	BALANCE:	BALANCE:	BALANCE:
BALANCE:	BALANCE:	BALANCE:	BALANCE:
BALANCE:	BALANCE:	BALANCE:	BALANCE:

Useful for cashflow planning. Plan your income and major bills & expenses throughout the month and record your daily projected balances to ensure you have a balanced budget.

THURSDAY	FRIDAY	SATURDAY
BALANCE:	BALANCE:	BALANCE:
BALANCE:	BALANCE:	BALANCE:
BALANCE:	BALANCE:	BALANCE:
BALANCE:	BALANCE:	BALANCE:
BALANCE:	BALANCE:	BALANCE:

Monthly Zero-Based Budget Planner
Start with a FRESH budget each month!

Month:	
Year:	

>Use the Quick Start Budget to help get started but be sure to plan for the special expenses that you will incur this month.
>Use the Paycheck Budget Planner to help plan out your cash flow and which expenses will be covered by each paycheck.
>Use the Calendar Budget Planner to map out a visual of when your income and expenses will occur throughout the month.

Income	Date	Planned	Actual
Total Income:			

NOTES

Basic Living Expenses			
Expense	**Date**	**Planned**	**Actual**
Food			
Home			
Utilities			
Transportation			
Total Basic Expenses			

Other Expenses			
Expense	**Date**	**Planned**	**Actual**
Giving			
Savings			
Other			
Debts			
Total Other Expenses			

Zero-Based Budget: A plan for every dollar

Total Income = Total Expenses

Any extra money in the budget should be applied towards debt, savings, and other goals that you have set.

Debt Snapshot	
Starting Balance	
Ending Balance	
Paid Off:	

Savings Snapshot	
Starting Balance	
Ending Balance	
Total Saved:	

PAYCHECK BUDGET

Useful for cashflow planning. Plan your expenses to be covered by certain paychecks to have an even cashflow throughout the month.

MONTH: **YEAR:**

Income	Exp. Date	Expected Amount	Actual	Difference
Paycheck 1				
Paycheck 2				
Paycheck 3				
Total Income:				

Paycheck 1 Expenses	Due Date	Budget	Actual	Difference
Subtotal Expenses:				

Paycheck 2 Expenses	Due Date	Budget	Actual	Difference
Subtotal Expenses:				

Paycheck 3 Expenses	Due Date	Budget	Actual	Difference
Subtotal Expenses:				

| **Total Expenses (All Subtotals):** | | | | |
| **Month End Balance (=Income - Expenses):** | | | | |

CALENDAR BUDGET

MONTH:

YEAR:

SUNDAY	MONDAY	TUESDAY	WEDNESDAY
BALANCE:	BALANCE:	BALANCE:	BALANCE:
BALANCE:	BALANCE:	BALANCE:	BALANCE:
BALANCE:	BALANCE:	BALANCE:	BALANCE:
BALANCE:	BALANCE:	BALANCE:	BALANCE:
BALANCE:	BALANCE:	BALANCE:	BALANCE:

Useful for cashflow planning. Plan your income and major bills & expenses throughout the month and record your daily projected balances to ensure you have a balanced budget.

THURSDAY	FRIDAY	SATURDAY
BALANCE:	BALANCE:	BALANCE:
BALANCE:	BALANCE:	BALANCE:
BALANCE:	BALANCE:	BALANCE:
BALANCE:	BALANCE:	BALANCE:
BALANCE:	BALANCE:	BALANCE:

Monthly Zero-Based Budget Planner

Start with a FRESH budget each month!

Month:	
Year:	

>Use the Quick Start Budget to help get started but be sure to plan for the special expenses that you will incur this month.
>Use the Paycheck Budget Planner to help plan out your cash flow and which expenses will be covered by each paycheck.
>Use the Calendar Budget Planner to map out a visual of when your income and expenses will occur throughout the month.

Income	Date	Planned	Actual
Total Income:			

NOTES

Basic Living Expenses

Expense	Date	Planned	Actual
Food			
Home			
Utilities			
Transportation			
Total Basic Expenses			

Other Expenses

Expense	Date	Planned	Actual
Giving			
Savings			
Other			
Debts			
Total Other Expenses			

Zero-Based Budget: A plan for every dollar

Total Income = Total Expenses

Any extra money in the budget should be applied towards debt, savings, and other goals that you have set.

Debt Snapshot

Starting Balance	
Ending Balance	
Paid Off:	

Savings Snapshot

Starting Balance	
Ending Balance	
Total Saved:	

PAYCHECK BUDGET

Useful for cashflow planning. Plan your expenses to be covered by certain paychecks to have an even cashflow throughout the month.

MONTH:

YEAR:

Income	Exp. Date	Expected Amount	Actual	Difference
Paycheck 1				
Paycheck 2				
Paycheck 3				
Total Income:				

Paycheck 1 Expenses	Due Date	Budget	Actual	Difference
Subtotal Expenses:				

Paycheck 2 Expenses	Due Date	Budget	Actual	Difference
Subtotal Expenses:				

Paycheck 3 Expenses	Due Date	Budget	Actual	Difference
Subtotal Expenses:				
Total Expenses (All Subtotals):				
Month End Balance (=Income - Expenses):				

CALENDAR BUDGET

MONTH: **YEAR:**

SUNDAY	MONDAY	TUESDAY	WEDNESDAY
BALANCE:	BALANCE:	BALANCE:	BALANCE:
BALANCE:	BALANCE:	BALANCE:	BALANCE:
BALANCE:	BALANCE:	BALANCE:	BALANCE:
BALANCE:	BALANCE:	BALANCE:	BALANCE:
BALANCE:	BALANCE:	BALANCE:	BALANCE:

Useful for cashflow planning. Plan your income and major bills & expenses throughout the month and record your daily projected balances to ensure you have a balanced budget.

NOTES

THURSDAY	FRIDAY	SATURDAY
BALANCE:	BALANCE:	BALANCE:
BALANCE:	BALANCE:	BALANCE:
BALANCE:	BALANCE:	BALANCE:
BALANCE:	BALANCE:	BALANCE:
BALANCE:	BALANCE:	BALANCE:

Monthly Zero-Based Budget Planner

Start with a FRESH budget each month!

Month:

Year:

>Use the Quick Start Budget to help get started but be sure to plan for the special expenses that you will incur this month.
>Use the Paycheck Budget Planner to help plan out your cash flow and which expenses will be covered by each paycheck.
>Use the Calendar Budget Planner to map out a visual of when your income and expenses will occur throughout the month.

Income	Date	Planned	Actual
Total Income:			

NOTES

Basic Living Expenses

Expense	Date	Planned	Actual
Food			
Home			
Utilities			
Transportation			
Total Basic Expenses			

Other Expenses

Expense	Date	Planned	Actual
Giving			
Savings			
Other			
Debts			
Total Other Expenses			

Zero-Based Budget: A plan for every dollar

Total Income = Total Expenses

Any extra money in the budget should be applied towards debt, savings, and other goals that you have set.

Debt Snapshot

Starting Balance	
Ending Balance	
Paid Off:	

Savings Snapshot

Starting Balance	
Ending Balance	
Total Saved:	

PAYCHECK BUDGET

Useful for cashflow planning. Plan your expenses to be covered by certain paychecks to have an even cashflow throughout the month.

MONTH:

YEAR:

Income	Exp. Date	Expected Amount	Actual	Difference
Paycheck 1				
Paycheck 2				
Paycheck 3				
Total Income:				

Paycheck 1 Expenses	Due Date	Budget	Actual	Difference
Subtotal Expenses:				

Paycheck 2 Expenses	Due Date	Budget	Actual	Difference
Subtotal Expenses:				

Paycheck 3 Expenses	Due Date	Budget	Actual	Difference
Subtotal Expenses:				
Total Expenses (All Subtotals):				
Month End Balance (=Income - Expenses):				

CALENDAR BUDGET

MONTH:

YEAR:

SUNDAY	MONDAY	TUESDAY	WEDNESDAY
BALANCE:	BALANCE:	BALANCE:	BALANCE:
BALANCE:	BALANCE:	BALANCE:	BALANCE:
BALANCE:	BALANCE:	BALANCE:	BALANCE:
BALANCE:	BALANCE:	BALANCE:	BALANCE:
BALANCE:	BALANCE:	BALANCE:	BALANCE:

Useful for cashflow planning. Plan your income and major bills & expenses throughout the month and record your daily projected balances to ensure you have a balanced budget.

NOTES

THURSDAY	FRIDAY	SATURDAY
BALANCE:	BALANCE:	BALANCE:
BALANCE:	BALANCE:	BALANCE:
BALANCE:	BALANCE:	BALANCE:
BALANCE:	BALANCE:	BALANCE:
BALANCE:	BALANCE:	BALANCE:

Monthly Zero-Based Budget Planner
Start with a FRESH budget each month!

Month:	
Year:	

>Use the Quick Start Budget to help get started but be sure to plan for the special expenses that you will incur this month.
>Use the Paycheck Budget Planner to help plan out your cash flow and which expenses will be covered by each paycheck.
>Use the Calendar Budget Planner to map out a visual of when your income and expenses will occur throughout the month.

Income	Date	Planned	Actual
Total Income:			

NOTES

Basic Living Expenses

Expense	Date	Planned	Actual
Food			
Home			
Utilities			
Transportation			
Total Basic Expenses			

Other Expenses

Expense	Date	Planned	Actual
Giving			
Savings			
Other			
Debts			
Total Other Expenses		

Zero-Based Budget: A plan for every dollar

Total Income = Total Expenses

Any extra money in the budget should be applied towards debt, savings, and other goals that you have set.

Debt Snapshot

Starting Balance	
Ending Balance	
Paid Off:	

Savings Snapshot

Starting Balance	
Ending Balance	
Total Saved:	

PAYCHECK BUDGET

Useful for cashflow planning. Plan your expenses to be covered by certain paychecks to have an even cashflow throughout the month.

MONTH: **YEAR:**

Income	Exp. Date	Expected Amount	Actual	Difference
Paycheck 1				
Paycheck 2				
Paycheck 3				
Total Income:				

Paycheck 1 Expenses	Due Date	Budget	Actual	Difference
Subtotal Expenses:				

Paycheck 2 Expenses	Due Date	Budget	Actual	Difference
Subtotal Expenses:				

Paycheck 3 Expenses	Due Date	Budget	Actual	Difference
Subtotal Expenses:				

Total Expenses (All Subtotals):				
Month End Balance (=Income - Expenses):				

CALENDAR BUDGET

MONTH: **YEAR:**

SUNDAY	MONDAY	TUESDAY	WEDNESDAY
BALANCE:	BALANCE:	BALANCE:	BALANCE:
BALANCE:	BALANCE:	BALANCE:	BALANCE:
BALANCE:	BALANCE:	BALANCE:	BALANCE:
BALANCE:	BALANCE:	BALANCE:	BALANCE:
BALANCE:	BALANCE:	BALANCE:	BALANCE:

Useful for cashflow planning. Plan your income and major bills & expenses throughout the month and record your daily projected balances to ensure you have a balanced budget.

THURSDAY	FRIDAY	SATURDAY
BALANCE:	BALANCE:	BALANCE:
BALANCE:	BALANCE:	BALANCE:
BALANCE:	BALANCE:	BALANCE:
BALANCE:	BALANCE:	BALANCE:
BALANCE:	BALANCE:	BALANCE:

Monthly Zero-Based Budget Planner
Start with a FRESH budget each month!

Month:	
Year:	

>Use the Quick Start Budget to help get started but be sure to plan for the special expenses that you will incur this month.
>Use the Paycheck Budget Planner to help plan out your cash flow and which expenses will be covered by each paycheck.
>Use the Calendar Budget Planner to map out a visual of when your income and expenses will occur throughout the month.

Income	Date	Planned	Actual
Total Income:			

NOTES

Basic Living Expenses					Other Expenses			
Expense	**Date**	**Planned**	**Actual**		**Expense**	**Date**	**Planned**	**Actual**
Food					Giving			
					Savings			
Home					Other			
Utilities								
Transportation					Debts			
Total Basic Expenses								

Zero-Based Budget: A plan for every dollar

Total Income = Total Expenses

Any extra money in the budget should be applied towards debt, savings, and other goals that you have set.

Total Other Expenses		

Debt Snapshot	
Starting Balance	
Ending Balance	
Paid Off:	

Savings Snapshot	
Starting Balance	
Ending Balance	
Total Saved:	

PAYCHECK BUDGET

Useful for cashflow planning. Plan your expenses to be covered by certain paychecks to have an even cashflow throughout the month.

MONTH: **YEAR:**

Income	Exp. Date	Expected Amount	Actual	Difference
Paycheck 1				
Paycheck 2				
Paycheck 3				
Total Income:				

Paycheck 1 Expenses	Due Date	Budget	Actual	Difference
Subtotal Expenses:				

Paycheck 2 Expenses	Due Date	Budget	Actual	Difference
Subtotal Expenses:				

Paycheck 3 Expenses	Due Date	Budget	Actual	Difference
Subtotal Expenses:				
Total Expenses (All Subtotals):				
Month End Balance (=Income - Expenses):				

CALENDAR BUDGET

MONTH: **YEAR:**

SUNDAY	MONDAY	TUESDAY	WEDNESDAY
BALANCE:	BALANCE:	BALANCE:	BALANCE:
BALANCE:	BALANCE:	BALANCE:	BALANCE:
BALANCE:	BALANCE:	BALANCE:	BALANCE:
BALANCE:	BALANCE:	BALANCE:	BALANCE:
BALANCE:	BALANCE:	BALANCE:	BALANCE:

Useful for cashflow planning. Plan your income and major bills & expenses throughout the month and record your daily projected balances to ensure you have a balanced budget.

THURSDAY	FRIDAY	SATURDAY
BALANCE:	BALANCE:	BALANCE:
BALANCE:	BALANCE:	BALANCE:
BALANCE:	BALANCE:	BALANCE:
BALANCE:	BALANCE:	BALANCE:
BALANCE:	BALANCE:	BALANCE:

Monthly Zero-Based Budget Planner
Start with a FRESH budget each month!

Month:

Year:

>Use the Quick Start Budget to help get started but be sure to plan for the special expenses that you will incur this month.
>Use the Paycheck Budget Planner to help plan out your cash flow and which expenses will be covered by each paycheck.
>Use the Calendar Budget Planner to map out a visual of when your income and expenses will occur throughout the month.

Income	Date	Planned	Actual
Total Income:			

NOTES

Basic Living Expenses			
Expense	**Date**	**Planned**	**Actual**
Food			
Home			
Utilities			
Transportation			
Total Basic Expenses			

Other Expenses			
Expense	**Date**	**Planned**	**Actual**
Giving			
Savings			
Other			
Debts			
Total Other Expenses		

Zero-Based Budget: A plan for every dollar

Total Income = Total Expenses

Any extra money in the budget should be applied towards debt, savings, and other goals that you have set.

Debt Snapshot	
Starting Balance	
Ending Balance	
Paid Off:	

Savings Snapshot	
Starting Balance	
Ending Balance	
Total Saved:	

PAYCHECK BUDGET

Useful for cashflow planning. Plan your expenses to be covered by certain paychecks to have an even cashflow throughout the month.

MONTH: **YEAR:**

Income	Exp. Date	Expected Amount	Actual	Difference
Paycheck 1				
Paycheck 2				
Paycheck 3				
Total Income:				

Paycheck 1 Expenses	Due Date	Budget	Actual	Difference
Subtotal Expenses:				

Paycheck 2 Expenses	Due Date	Budget	Actual	Difference
Subtotal Expenses:				

Paycheck 3 Expenses	Due Date	Budget	Actual	Difference
Subtotal Expenses:				

Total Expenses (All Subtotals):				
Month End Balance (=Income - Expenses):				

CALENDAR BUDGET

MONTH: **YEAR:**

SUNDAY	MONDAY	TUESDAY	WEDNESDAY
BALANCE:	BALANCE:	BALANCE:	BALANCE:
BALANCE:	BALANCE:	BALANCE:	BALANCE:
BALANCE:	BALANCE:	BALANCE:	BALANCE:
BALANCE:	BALANCE:	BALANCE:	BALANCE:
BALANCE:	BALANCE:	BALANCE:	BALANCE:

Useful for cashflow planning. Plan your income and major bills & expenses throughout the month and record your daily projected balances to ensure you have a balanced budget.

THURSDAY	FRIDAY	SATURDAY
BALANCE:	BALANCE:	BALANCE:
BALANCE:	BALANCE:	BALANCE:
BALANCE:	BALANCE:	BALANCE:
BALANCE:	BALANCE:	BALANCE:
BALANCE:	BALANCE:	BALANCE:

Monthly Zero-Based Budget Planner
Start with a FRESH budget each month!

Month:	
Year:	

>Use the Quick Start Budget to help get started but be sure to plan for the special expenses that you will incur this month.
>Use the Paycheck Budget Planner to help plan out your cash flow and which expenses will be covered by each paycheck.
>Use the Calendar Budget Planner to map out a visual of when your income and expenses will occur throughout the month.

Income	Date	Planned	Actual
Total Income:			

NOTES

Basic Living Expenses			
Expense	**Date**	**Planned**	**Actual**
Food			
Home			
Utilities			
Transportation			
Total Basic Expenses			

Other Expenses			
Expense	**Date**	**Planned**	**Actual**
Giving			
Savings			
Other			
Debts			
Total Other Expenses			

Zero-Based Budget: A plan for every dollar

Total Income = Total Expenses

Any extra money in the budget should be applied towards debt, savings, and other goals that you have set.

Debt Snapshot	
Starting Balance	
Ending Balance	
Paid Off:	

Savings Snapshot	
Starting Balance	
Ending Balance	
Total Saved:	

PAYCHECK BUDGET

Useful for cashflow planning. Plan your expenses to be covered by certain paychecks to have an even cashflow throughout the month.

MONTH:

YEAR:

Income	Exp. Date	Expected Amount	Actual	Difference
Paycheck 1				
Paycheck 2				
Paycheck 3				
Total Income:				

Paycheck 1 Expenses	Due Date	Budget	Actual	Difference
Subtotal Expenses:				

Paycheck 2 Expenses	Due Date	Budget	Actual	Difference
Subtotal Expenses:				

Paycheck 3 Expenses	Due Date	Budget	Actual	Difference
Subtotal Expenses:				

| **Total Expenses (All Subtotals):** | | | | |
| **Month End Balance (=Income - Expenses):** | | | | |

CALENDAR BUDGET

MONTH: **YEAR:**

SUNDAY	MONDAY	TUESDAY	WEDNESDAY
BALANCE:	BALANCE:	BALANCE:	BALANCE:
BALANCE:	BALANCE:	BALANCE:	BALANCE:
BALANCE:	BALANCE:	BALANCE:	BALANCE:
BALANCE:	BALANCE:	BALANCE:	BALANCE:
BALANCE:	BALANCE:	BALANCE:	BALANCE:

Useful for cashflow planning. Plan your income and major bills & expenses throughout the month and record your daily projected balances to ensure you have a balanced budget.

NOTES

THURSDAY	FRIDAY	SATURDAY
BALANCE:	BALANCE:	BALANCE:
BALANCE:	BALANCE:	BALANCE:
BALANCE:	BALANCE:	BALANCE:
BALANCE:	BALANCE:	BALANCE:
BALANCE:	BALANCE:	BALANCE:

2018

January

S	M	T	W	T	F	S
	1	2	3	4	5	6
7	8	9	10	11	12	13
14	15	16	17	18	19	20
21	22	23	24	25	26	27
28	29	30	31			

February

S	M	T	W	T	F	S
				1	2	3
4	5	6	7	8	9	10
11	12	13	14	15	16	17
18	19	20	21	22	23	24
25	26	27	28			

March

S	M	T	W	T	F	S
				1	2	3
4	5	6	7	8	9	10
11	12	13	14	15	16	17
18	19	20	21	22	23	24
25	26	27	28	29	30	31

April

S	M	T	W	T	F	S
1	2	3	4	5	6	7
8	9	10	11	12	13	14
15	16	17	18	19	20	21
22	23	24	25	26	27	28
29	30					

May

S	M	T	W	T	F	S
		1	2	3	4	5
6	7	8	9	10	11	12
13	14	15	16	17	18	19
20	21	22	23	24	25	26
27	28	29	30	31		

June

S	M	T	W	T	F	S
					1	2
3	4	5	6	7	8	9
10	11	12	13	14	15	16
17	18	19	20	21	22	23
24	25	26	27	28	29	30

July

S	M	T	W	T	F	S
1	2	3	4	5	6	7
8	9	10	11	12	13	14
15	16	17	18	19	20	21
22	23	24	25	26	27	28
29	30	31				

August

S	M	T	W	T	F	S
			1	2	3	4
5	6	7	8	9	10	11
12	13	14	15	16	17	18
19	20	21	22	23	24	25
26	27	28	29	30	31	

September

S	M	T	W	T	F	S
						1
2	3	4	5	6	7	8
9	10	11	12	13	14	15
16	17	18	19	20	21	22
23	24	25	26	27	28	29
30						

October

S	M	T	W	T	F	S
	1	2	3	4	5	6
7	8	9	10	11	12	13
14	15	16	17	18	19	20
21	22	23	24	25	26	27
28	29	30	31			

November

S	M	T	W	T	F	S
				1	2	3
4	5	6	7	8	9	10
11	12	13	14	15	16	17
18	19	20	21	22	23	24
25	26	27	28	29	30	

December

S	M	T	W	T	F	S
						1
2	3	4	5	6	7	8
9	10	11	12	13	14	15
16	17	18	19	20	21	22
23	24	25	26	27	28	29
30	31					

2019

January
S	M	T	W	T	F	S
		1	2	3	4	5
6	7	8	9	10	11	12
13	14	15	16	17	18	19
20	21	22	23	24	25	26
27	28	29	30	31		

February
S	M	T	W	T	F	S
					1	2
3	4	5	6	7	8	9
10	11	12	13	14	15	16
17	18	19	20	21	22	23
24	25	26	27	28		

March
S	M	T	W	T	F	S
					1	2
3	4	5	6	7	8	9
10	11	12	13	14	15	16
17	18	19	20	21	22	23
24	25	26	27	28	29	30
31						

April
S	M	T	W	T	F	S
	1	2	3	4	5	6
7	8	9	10	11	12	13
14	15	16	17	18	19	20
21	22	23	24	25	26	27
28	29	30				

May
S	M	T	W	T	F	S
			1	2	3	4
5	6	7	8	9	10	11
12	13	14	15	16	17	18
19	20	21	22	23	24	25
26	27	28	29	30	31	

June
S	M	T	W	T	F	S
						1
2	3	4	5	6	7	8
9	10	11	12	13	14	15
16	17	18	19	20	21	22
23	24	25	26	27	28	29
30						

July
S	M	T	W	T	F	S
	1	2	3	4	5	6
7	8	9	10	11	12	13
14	15	16	17	18	19	20
21	22	23	24	25	26	27
28	29	30	31			

August
S	M	T	W	T	F	S
				1	2	3
4	5	6	7	8	9	10
11	12	13	14	15	16	17
18	19	20	21	22	23	24
25	26	27	28	29	30	31

September
S	M	T	W	T	F	S
1	2	3	4	5	6	7
8	9	10	11	12	13	14
15	16	17	18	19	20	21
22	23	24	25	26	27	28
29	30					

October
S	M	T	W	T	F	S
		1	2	3	4	5
6	7	8	9	10	11	12
13	14	15	16	17	18	19
20	21	22	23	24	25	26
27	28	29	30	31		

November
S	M	T	W	T	F	S
					1	2
3	4	5	6	7	8	9
10	11	12	13	14	15	16
17	18	19	20	21	22	23
24	25	26	27	28	29	30

December
S	M	T	W	T	F	S
1	2	3	4	5	6	7
8	9	10	11	12	13	14
15	16	17	18	19	20	21
22	23	24	25	26	27	28
29	30	31				

2020

January

S	M	T	W	T	F	S
		1	2	3	4	
5	6	7	8	9	10	11
12	13	14	15	16	17	18
19	20	21	22	23	24	25
26	27	28	29	30	31	

February

S	M	T	W	T	F	S
						1
2	3	4	5	6	7	8
9	10	11	12	13	14	15
16	17	18	19	20	21	22
23	24	25	26	27	28	29

March

S	M	T	W	T	F	S
1	2	3	4	5	6	7
8	9	10	11	12	13	14
15	16	17	18	19	20	21
22	23	24	25	26	27	28
29	30	31				

April

S	M	T	W	T	F	S
		1	2	3	4	
5	6	7	8	9	10	11
12	13	14	15	16	17	18
19	20	21	22	23	24	25
26	27	28	29	30		

May

S	M	T	W	T	F	S
					1	2
3	4	5	6	7	8	9
10	11	12	13	14	15	16
17	18	19	20	21	22	23
24	25	26	27	28	29	30
31						

June

S	M	T	W	T	F	S
	1	2	3	4	5	6
7	8	9	10	11	12	13
14	15	16	17	18	19	20
21	22	23	24	25	26	27
28	29	30				

July

S	M	T	W	T	F	S
		1	2	3	4	
5	6	7	8	9	10	11
12	13	14	15	16	17	18
19	20	21	22	23	24	25
26	27	28	29	30	31	

August

S	M	T	W	T	F	S
						1
2	3	4	5	6	7	8
9	10	11	12	13	14	15
16	17	18	19	20	21	22
23	24	25	26	27	28	29
30	31					

September

S	M	T	W	T	F	S
		1	2	3	4	5
6	7	8	9	10	11	12
13	14	15	16	17	18	19
20	21	22	23	24	25	26
27	28	29	30			

October

S	M	T	W	T	F	S
				1	2	3
4	5	6	7	8	9	10
11	12	13	14	15	16	17
18	19	20	21	22	23	24
25	26	27	28	29	30	31

November

S	M	T	W	T	F	S
1	2	3	4	5	6	7
8	9	10	11	12	13	14
15	16	17	18	19	20	21
22	23	24	25	26	27	28
29	30					

December

S	M	T	W	T	F	S
		1	2	3	4	5
6	7	8	9	10	11	12
13	14	15	16	17	18	19
20	21	22	23	24	25	26
27	28	29	30	31		

2021

January
S	M	T	W	T	F	S
					1	2
3	4	5	6	7	8	9
10	11	12	13	14	15	16
17	18	19	20	21	22	23
24	25	26	27	28	29	30
31						

February
S	M	T	W	T	F	S
	1	2	3	4	5	6
7	8	9	10	11	12	13
14	15	16	17	18	19	20
21	22	23	24	25	26	27
28						

March
S	M	T	W	T	F	S
	1	2	3	4	5	6
7	8	9	10	11	12	13
14	15	16	17	18	19	20
21	22	23	24	25	26	27
28	29	30	31			

April
S	M	T	W	T	F	S
				1	2	3
4	5	6	7	8	9	10
11	12	13	14	15	16	17
18	19	20	21	22	23	24
25	26	27	28	29	30	

May
S	M	T	W	T	F	S
						1
2	3	4	5	6	7	8
9	10	11	12	13	14	15
16	17	18	19	20	21	22
23	24	25	26	27	28	29
30	31					

June
S	M	T	W	T	F	S
		1	2	3	4	5
6	7	8	9	10	11	12
13	14	15	16	17	18	19
20	21	22	23	24	25	26
27	28	29	30			

July
S	M	T	W	T	F	S
				1	2	3
4	5	6	7	8	9	10
11	12	13	14	15	16	17
18	19	20	21	22	23	24
25	26	27	28	29	30	31

August
S	M	T	W	T	F	S
1	2	3	4	5	6	7
8	9	10	11	12	13	14
15	16	17	18	19	20	21
22	23	24	25	26	27	28
29	30	31				

September
S	M	T	W	T	F	S
			1	2	3	4
5	6	7	8	9	10	11
12	13	14	15	16	17	18
19	20	21	22	23	24	25
26	27	28	29	30		

October
S	M	T	W	T	F	S
					1	2
3	4	5	6	7	8	9
10	11	12	13	14	15	16
17	18	19	20	21	22	23
24	25	26	27	28	29	30
31						

November
S	M	T	W	T	F	S
	1	2	3	4	5	6
7	8	9	10	11	12	13
14	15	16	17	18	19	20
21	22	23	24	25	26	27
28	29	30				

December
S	M	T	W	T	F	S
			1	2	3	4
5	6	7	8	9	10	11
12	13	14	15	16	17	18
19	20	21	22	23	24	25
26	27	28	29	30	31	

2022

January
S	M	T	W	T	F	S
						1
2	3	4	5	6	7	8
9	10	11	12	13	14	15
16	17	18	19	20	21	22
23	24	25	26	27	28	29
30	31					

February
S	M	T	W	T	F	S
		1	2	3	4	5
6	7	8	9	10	11	12
13	14	15	16	17	18	19
20	21	22	23	24	25	26
27	28					

March
S	M	T	W	T	F	S
		1	2	3	4	5
6	7	8	9	10	11	12
13	14	15	16	17	18	19
20	21	22	23	24	25	26
27	28	29	30	31		

April
S	M	T	W	T	F	S
					1	2
3	4	5	6	7	8	9
10	11	12	13	14	15	16
17	18	19	20	21	22	23
24	25	26	27	28	29	30

May
S	M	T	W	T	F	S
1	2	3	4	5	6	7
8	9	10	11	12	13	14
15	16	17	18	19	20	21
22	23	24	25	26	27	28
29	30	31				

June
S	M	T	W	T	F	S
			1	2	3	4
5	6	7	8	9	10	11
12	13	14	15	16	17	18
19	20	21	22	23	24	25
26	27	28	29	30		

July
S	M	T	W	T	F	S
					1	2
3	4	5	6	7	8	9
10	11	12	13	14	15	16
17	18	19	20	21	22	23
24	25	26	27	28	29	30
31						

August
S	M	T	W	T	F	S
	1	2	3	4	5	6
7	8	9	10	11	12	13
14	15	16	17	18	19	20
21	22	23	24	25	26	27
28	29	30	31			

September
S	M	T	W	T	F	S
				1	2	3
4	5	6	7	8	9	10
11	12	13	14	15	16	17
18	19	20	21	22	23	24
25	26	27	28	29	30	

October
S	M	T	W	T	F	S
						1
2	3	4	5	6	7	8
9	10	11	12	13	14	15
16	17	18	19	20	21	22
23	24	25	26	27	28	29
30	31					

November
S	M	T	W	T	F	S
		1	2	3	4	5
6	7	8	9	10	11	12
13	14	15	16	17	18	19
20	21	22	23	24	25	26
27	28	29	30			

December
S	M	T	W	T	F	S
				1	2	3
4	5	6	7	8	9	10
11	12	13	14	15	16	17
18	19	20	21	22	23	24
25	26	27	28	29	30	31

Made in the USA
Columbia, SC
10 February 2019